33 W

Water

Dawn Clutter

BookLeaf
Publishing

Presentation by *BookLeaf Publishing*

Web: www.bookleafpub.com

E-mail: info@bookleafpub.com

ISBN: 9789357618311

First edition 2022

For my Mom, who was always my biggest fan.

ACKNOWLEDGEMENT

Shout out to all my friends who ever read my crap and humored me with compliments. You da best ;)

Also, I want to thank teachers. They change the way a person grasps language and helps them love it or hate it. The ones who made me love it: Kennedy, Bergmooser, and Dillon. You can't know the impact you had on my brain.

PREFACE

If I had a dime for every time someone told me, "you should write a book!," I wouldn't need to write this book.

But instead of telling you my story (maybe someday), I'll go one step further. I'll let you dive a little deeper... my story would only tell you facts and events. My poems will tell you how those facts and events changed me.

1 Way to Look at Water

"Carry my flip-flops," I said, carelessly,
as I trotted down to the edge
where wet meets dry,
gills meet lungs,
dark meets light.

I was never much of a swimmer.

When I was a child,
my daddy lifted me high
over his head, always
before I was ready, and
threw my tiny toddler body
high and far and away.

I always came up
sputtering and choking,
snot running down my chin,
and I cried.

I cried because I never saw it coming, and
I tried because I wanted to please him, and
to this day, I have to hold my nose to go under.

I giggled at you, standing on the shore,
my flip-flops in hand, just grinning

with your dirty
thoughts of sin;
I said, "come in."

I was never much of a teaser.

When I was a teen,
a boy I went to school with
went swimming late at night
in a lake red from the moon,
so red, it was black. It stole him;
it never gave him back.

He often comes up
in my watery dreams
and improper moments
like right now.

I don't go deeper than my waistline; I can't, and
I won't stay in past the red setting sun, and
to this day, I have to hold my heart to go under.

I don't need to say it, but I still do:
"I love that you love that I love you,
and my flip-flops,
safe on shore?
They love you, too."

I was never much a romantic.

When I was full grown,
I took swimming lessons.
I learned to dive right in
and fight my way to the top.
Nobody else throws me in; I
throw myself with vigor.

But now, here we are,
and we're in deep water.
Wrapping my legs around
you, we swim.

We love because we never saw it coming, and
we will not regret a thing that we've done, and
from this day, I want to hold your hand to go
under.

Caffiend

Street-dealer Bobby drove a Denali,
paint like a sleek, running panther in a wet oil
slick,
melting together like lovers with vampire-killing
silver rims and trims
and a thunder-kissed stereo, bass kicking, hard,
like the thump in your chest on a back street
with the 5-0 treading concrete in their black
patent boots,
and maybe, if they wore Nikes, they'd catch
you.
Fast cars, fast whores, fast money - Bobby liked
speed;
He blew his money faster than the crack heads
and coke fiends.
Living.
Living.
Living.

Bobby was a Trojan horse, a fighter, a
catch-me-if-you-can.
He had good looks and good hooks, but Bobby
was bad -
He sold and bought your daughters, wives, your
lawyers, and your priests.

It's true, brother - don't let down your beliefs -
this is America. We live. We die.
We choose what cover we're judged by.
If you don't pay the dollar, he'll take your DVD,
your VCR, your TV.
If that isn't enough, he'll trade for all three.

Bobby doesn't mind.

What about me? I'm just a junkie in my own
right.
I turn down the razors, needles, and pipes,
but, I still wake up at 6:05 to the smell of
crystallized coffee beans
and start my morning craving for killing tar and
nicotine,
and what would a Friday night be without some
good ol' JD
and a coke - whether diet or not - it don't matter
no more.
And on Saturday night, or Tuesday, whenever,
nothing's better than a roll in the hay, and I'm
always
Fiending.
Fiending.
Fiending.

And sometimes, late at night, while I'm chock
full of No-Doz,

I think of Bobby and all the powder he shoved in
his nose.
I think of the summers that Bobby and I kicked
it,
high on acid by the campfire, talking . . .

Can you dig it?

He told me he loved me once, but I only imagine
that he loved the way I made him feel higher
than his drugs,
higher than the kites that flew over the park
downtown,
where he pushed baggies to kids and took their
dollars for dimes.

Bobby didn't mind.

But, Bobby pulled a fast one, a quick trick, sold
to the man -
no sooner did he see the metal cuffs, Bobby ran.
The cops yelled freeze.
Bobby froze,
turned and faced his fears, his woes; his gun
screamed
and bullets run faster than any man.

Ask Bobby. He knows.

Cop shot, Bobby shot, both fell fast.
A trigger-happy street-thug dreamed of his past.
He dreamt of his future and the fact he didn't
have one,
like I dream of Bobby late into the summer
nights
like the ones when we used to hold tight
to one another. Now, I sleep alone, waiting for
Bobby.
Waiting.
Waiting.
Waiting.

Bobby healed, but not all wounds do.
The wounds in the children he sold to will fester
and boil
until they are adults, weeping for order,
weeping for all of their chaos to end
that is making them lose all their family and
friends.

Bobby never paid no mind.

Now, Bobby's doing time. Big time. Big house.
Big rules.
Bobby's gonna die, and he's not gonna die high.
He'll be more alive than you and I are alive,
but his skin will always breathe fumes of
intoxicants,

his blood will flow thicker than butter through
paper-thin veins,
and he'll be a dealer, a street-dealer, in his mind,
Forever.
Forever.
Forever.

Dandelion

Oh, pretty weed, looking
so at peace in my grass,
feeding off rain showers
from hazel skies and my
windswept leaves fallen from
trees – my yard never felt
so used and trod upon.

You throw parties, invite
matching friends to invade
and parade like yellow
sheep crawling through my veins,
bleeding with life, eating
wooden hearts, unpleasant
yellow-stained memories.

You grow, grow tall, and strong,
reaching calloused green hands
for the throat of the sun,
while I wither from lack
of heat and seed; I need
nourishment to just breathe
and thrive; you thieving weed.

Dirt patches scent the air,

as breeze blows reminders
of what once grew in fields,
now overrun, dying
like cornstalks in September,
like grandmothers when they
still made that sweet, warm wine.

I remember when wind
blew through tufts of your hair,
scattering love with each
breath that God gave to breathe;
now, with every breath,
however soft, you reach
for my throat, and you breed.

Fragments of Conversation

"I'd like roast beef on white with mayo,"
she said, or more to the truth,
she whispered,
hushed voice with her head down,
as if the calorie police were waiting
in the dark recesses of the carry-out,
past the overweight prep cook
and the lazy manager
on the telephone, saying
"she didn't mean anything to me,
honey; please stay;
please don't leave"
to a wife, or a girlfriend,
or a boyfriend if it pleases
the man who signs the checks
and orders paper bags
in which this woman's fattening sandwich
will be placed in her anorexic hands, as she flees
hurriedly,
into some dark recess
to gorge herself and purge.
"That'll be $6.36," the pimply cashier ordered
with outstretched palms,
while in the back of his head,
all he could remember

was his father's red, swollen face
telling him how he would never amount to
anything
but a fast-food clerk.
"Sit down and shut up,"
momma bear told baby bear,
while there was no daddy bear
    - anywhere -.
I wanted to tell that whiny brat
that his poppa probably left
because he wouldn't sit down
or shut up like momma bear had said.
 "I don't know how you can eat that crap," my
co-worker
pronounced, from just behind me, in line
to order the same crap that I was ordering,
although she would order hers
with low-fat honey mustard
and whole wheat
so she can go home and tell her husband
        (who doesn't care or love her anymore)
that she ate a healthy sandwich at lunch that day,
as if that healthy sandwich is going to erase her
overgrown ass
that hasn't stopped growing since three weeks
after
their post-marital,
half-hour coital engagement,
quasi-honeymoon

at the Holiday Inn.

I Took in Addiction

When I was an infant, I took my
momma's bottle in my mouth,
took in addiction like a vein
pumps blood, suckled until
my mother ran dry
like the dusty river bed
down the road, where, when I was older,
but young enough to think I knew
which way the wind was blowing,
I ran with boys and smoked cigarettes,
momma's brand, snuck from dark recesses
in hidden desk drawers. I took in addiction
and never exhaled into the wind
like a hurricane blowing westward,
leaving swirls of dust older than
my eighteen years into knowing
everything
and eighteen years into knowing
nothing.

I took my momma's bottle in my mouth,
stolen from dusty, cobwebbed cupboards
and hidden by the fire extinguisher,
momma's metaphor

for the fire that daddy put out, and
she kept lit;
oh... she kept lit.

I took in addiction like my daddy
took in women across town,
half his age and meaner than momma,
even when she had the fire burning
hot like black coals
hidden safely in that old cigar box I found
one day before running,
filled with still white coals
that momma hadn't
formed her metaphors for.
The yellow Bic laid in with the coals,
a burst of sunshine in a dusk-warmed sky,
deeper than twilight,
softer than midnight,
and I took in addiction
like a baby takes in coos
and ahhs and momma's bottle,
and I ran myself dry,
ran screaming into adulthood,
where I found the other side,
the side with moans in secret rooms
and promises of bliss and
all the white-trained princess dreams
that momma yarned,
and I fell into step beside her,

one addiction at a time;
I fell back behind her,
let her lead me to temptation,
where I finally found
it easy to let go
of her hand and rush head-first
into my own form of metaphors.

Rainbow

I moved through the flavors, one skittle at a
time,
diving inside strips of the rainbow to taste
the blues and greens and reds,
the white and gold and silver.
I ate hard-shells and soft-insides and pink tufts
of candied cotton dancing in the breeze. I fell
down
upon scarred knees in fields with lilac and
clover.

I never gave my taffy to the boy next door. He
stole it,
heaving and punching and threatening
with words and with fists.
He ran, laughing, and I moved on to the next
pasture
with honeybees swarming past my sweet taste,
my honey face, my happy tears, and teenage
angst.

When I looked into my mother's eyes
and saw her fear and loathing,
I swept my long hair back off my cheeks
and held my head high and ran, ran,

ran past rows of pine trees into the meadow
while the giant oak stood guard over the swollen
forest, fat with mystery and promise
of what one might seek down there.

I tasted every flavor, from lime to the lemon
to the sweetest cherry; I let them melt,
melt, melt onto my tongue, running in rainbows
of colors, swirling to new flavors of tomorrow
that could always leave me feeling that maybe,
maybe, maybe I could just be free
from all the colors that left my mother weeping.

Riding Bareback on a White Horse

My mother used to tell me tales of glue factories
while I sat at the kitchen table and used Elmer's
to paste together pictures
of Black Beauty
and Silver.

               I didn't care when I was six.

I cared about Barbie's Dream House,
and jumping rope,
and my father
in the other room,
       with a tourniquet
on his arm
       and a needle
in his vein.

He was always talkingtalkingtalking
on the phone with strangers
who stopped by in the
middle
of the night.

He worked hard at his glue factory; he must
have.

He was   always
tired,   always
slumped over   always
                          sleeping.

He was always runningrunningrunning
Sometimes he'd leave for   hours,

                                    days,
                                    weeks
                                    at a
time, and

when he eventually stopped coming home at all,
I asked my mother where he had gone.

She told me stories of white horses and fast
tracks
while I sat at the kitchen table with empty eyes
and dreamt dreams
of Black Beauty
and Silver.

Eventually, my father's white horse
stampeded and raged
through his heart
            the day before his fiftieth birthday,

20

and he held tight in his saddle
and gripped her
wet mane.

A View From the Parapet at Pharos

A seagull flies past Summer lights at sea
with rays from towers tall on rocky shores.
The sailor's ship with mast kidnapped by breeze,
and sailor scans with old binoculars.

He sees her figure on shore scanning back
and almost sees the tears she hides behind,
a lonely existence - she knows no friends.
This island's small and passed by tide and time.

Her dreams of love unanswered, yet, it sails
five hundred feet apart from him to her,
and prayers unneeded now, she dares to dream
that somehow, love's small ship has dared arrive.

The sailor's view obscured by white-capped
waves,
but yet, he sees himself within her dreams,
and she belongs in his remaining time.
He sends his love to her through seagull's
screams.

Alas! This dream will end for both their hearts -

the rocks are sharp; the sea's too fierce.
The danger's near, but simpler yet - their fear!
      His home's at sea; her home is here.

A twist of fate has sealed this tale of love,
this fleeting moment between sea and shore -
he sailed his ship and passed her by that night;
and she, a tower, lit the sailor's sea.

Rush Hour

The midnight rush at six p.m.,
stars shining bright in rearviews
and across median galaxies,
I sped light speed through meteors,
dodging comets to get to you.

The wail of sirens cut through thick
atmospheric pressure in my skull,
the cloudy flapping wipers smearing
mascara running through my milky way
of tears, and my foot falls.

I can't find you, out here, you hide
among the beasts of planets and tiny moons.
Like specks of DNA on a proton,
our feelings have become miniscule
and drowned out by the rest of the world.

If we were not the astronauts we are,
and we again knew the long days of Summer,
the cold, empty four-lane solar system
would not swallow me up whole
and spit you out into particles of memory.

Four Haikus

Paint dries slow on wall,
crumbling wallpaper fades
like the evening sun.

I remember days
when the colors were vibrant
and shining like new.

We need a new coat
more and more every year
because age does fade.

I prefer high gloss,
a coat of red or yellow
to hide the dark side.

11 Ways to Look at Water

"Dive," you said,
"dive into the deep
where the water is black;
I will be here when you get back."

So, I dove, headfirst,
arms stretched above me
in mountain pose,
body arched forward,
breath held; I dove far
and deep below the surface.

There, in the murky nothing,
I let myself drift,
rose slowly to the surface
where oxygen beckoned like a lover.

The water was frigid.
My bones ached; my lungs were tight;
gooseflesh rose on my skin,
everything froze but my heart.

I broke through into your arms,
caught in between cold and warm.
Together, we kicked and paddled

and climbed into the crisp autumn night.

There, in the cabin aft,
we curled into blankets and each other,
one hand wrapped around coffee,
one hand wrapped around yours.

"Dive," you said,
"dive into the deep
where the water is black;
I will be here when you get back."

So, I dove, headfirst into you,
arms stretched beneath you
in shavasana pose,
body arched backward,
breathe held; I dove far
and deep below the surface.

If a Memory Was Important, I Kept It

There's so much more to life than
being a hard worker or being rich.

Your death will come; expect it.

You are not what you see in the mirror;
You are what others see inside you.

Your looks will fade; accept it.

Who do you plan to leave behind?
Will you be remembered as someone who lived?
Or will you be forgotten in just a few years
because of all the things you never did?

Nobody remembers someone who worked
their fingers until they bled.
Nobody remembers someone who looked
beautiful when they were dead.

Life is about the travels you take
and seeing all there is to see;
there are mountains and rivers and forests
where you can stand and just BE.

Life is about leaving your mark,
perhaps a poem or a song.
It's about experiencing all you can...

We're not here long; don't neglect it.

Be a shining beacon in someone's dark;
you might help someone survive.
When a fire has died, be a spark
to keep those flames alive.

If anything is worth saving, respect it.

Hold convictions in all of your actions;
if it's a hill worth dying on, stand.
But, if someone is reaching with a logical mind,
you're not a coward if you take their hand.

But if someone mistreats you; dissect it.

Be wide awake, even when sleeping;
that doesn't mean be "woke."
Because honestly, telling everyone else how to
live,
well... that's a joke.

When you are long gone, and your name
remains,

be able to say you lived a life worth living.
For when people stand over your grave,
asking what you did with time you were given,

Don't let them say that you slept it.

The Last Time I Saw Her

From where my guilt laid, silent words
marinated
in blood and fear of aging bones and falling hair.

I saw your princess dress, tattered and torn,
your whispered flesh, stretched and worn
through
like a plastic cover on a bag of mulch.

I had seen the future.
It was a shade darker than the day before;
it was a shadow
that followed the past.

It was the last thing I saw before
I crossed my heart and hoped to die.

When young souls age, dreams are shuffled
off to hide in boxes piled high.
The garage is filled with trains and treats,
school, the sea, your first kiss, and
memories of your mother. She laughed once
at you, directly at you, and it hurt.

It burnt like a cigarette ash blown by the wind

into your eye before you could blink.

You felt wrath at the time; you hated her for
months.
You'd give anything to hear her laugh once
more.

On some days, God exists.
I can hear him in the whistle of the wind on the
waves
of the ocean when I travel there.
I then pray the Lord my soul to keep.

Other days, he is a character in a book.
I will close my eyes for the last time;
I will never look at the ocean again;
I will only be asleep.

If I Were

If I were a speck of dust, someone would
acknowledge that I am there
resting on the shiny walnut veneer of a corner
curio cabinet
where, inside, even the brittle china is stronger.

If I were a sunrise, you would know I have risen.
Would you also know
that I shine on the outside but burn hot and
hollow at my core?
I waste oxygen. I am not a tree.

If I were in a carnival side show, I would be the
stray cat
weaving in and out of the crowd with their
upward eyes.
I am the bearded woman, freshly shaved.
I am the elephant man in a mask.

If I were in a movie, I would be a cameo.
I would have one line,
but I would be heard.

If I were an ant, my life would have been over
long ago.

No foot would ever notice my small black body
seeking a thousand pound reason to keep
moving on.

If I were an heirloom, I could sit at the table of
my family
and fit in. I would be welcome there, like the
pumpkin pie.

If I were an acrobat, at least I would be brave,
for the sound of falling has left my empty ears.
Like too many freight trains passing in the night,
I am deaf. I am mute. I am silence.

If I were you, I would not see me. I would taste
the dew in the air,
hear the whispering brush of the wind, see the
flames of a thousand fires,
but I would still have no name.

If I were a God, I would say, "do not cower
before the King
if you cannot acknowledge the existence of
every molecule of my heart."

If I were as important as a molecule, I would
belong there.

Flight 2122

Flight 2122

He walks through the gate
wearing tinted sunglasses
and dark un-tanned skin.

He smiles a warm smile,
says, "It's been awhile, my friend,"
and stretches his arms.

Summer then greets Spring,
embraces him and says,
"I'll see you next year."

Autumn then arrives.
She's an exhibitionist
shedding her clothing.

She shies from Summer.
Autumn is smitten and
pining for Winter.

But, when Winter comes,
Autumn is too cold;
she runs naked and embarrassed.

Winter loves herself;
she has no need for Autumn
and shoos her away.

Winter has arrived.
She carries icy luggage
for her round-trip flight.

With a bitter smile,
she greets you with cold kisses
and hands you her bags.

Another jet comes
flying in with icicles.
They melt; Spring is here.

He is the father
of those who create life, and
flowers are blooming.

Spring says his good-byes
to Winter, sends her away
and waits for Summer.

The gate calls boarding,
and another flight departs -
            four destinations.
Three months will pass 'til next time.

They will never travel together.

The Sunburn Memory

Once, when I was a young teen
living in the sunshine state,
my mom and I went to the beach,
a mother/daughter day.

She took off walking down the shore,
left me sleeping on a bed of sand
where I drifted off in a wave of heat,
head resting on my hands.

When she returned from her adventure,
hands full of rinsed-off shells,
I awoke to a wave of pain
and her loudly worried yells.

Florida sun will blister skin
and burn you like no other.
I knew it was bad when I saw
the expression of my mother.

I began to feel the pain of welts,
large blisters over beet-red skin;
they covered my entire back,
filled with water to save the raw within.

From there, we walked gently to the car,
each step more agonizing than the last,
and I crawled in on my belly first,
and my mother hit the gas.

She headed home, and all I felt
was a pounding in my head.
In retrospect, we should have gone
to the hospital instead.

For days, I laid on my stomach,
tender flesh laid open to the air,
while mother put aloe constantly
on a pain so hard to bear.

Eventually, I healed in time,
forgot the severity of my burn,
and I still love the sun; I still lay out
and I've still not quite yet learned.

But, my mother is no longer there
to save me from the sun.
The scars that cover my whole back,
they're not the only ones.

I also have some scars inside
that just won't go away,
and a memory can burn more than sun,

as does my memory of that day.

U

I am a No. 2 pencil in a new box of twelve.
I am a grain of sand on a random beach.
I am a rock on the ledge of the Grand Canyon
and on the shore of the Caspian Sea.

I am aqua and cyan and turquoise and teal;
I might even be powder and sky,
and I am a wrinkle on an elephant's skin,
but never the one who rides.

I am a goldfish in a backyard pond.
I am a ring in an ancient tree.
I am A and E and I, O, U;
I am even X, Y, Z.

I wish someone would sharpen my lead
and carry me in on their dampened feet,
throw me into the air, making a wish,
or skip me on water... 1... 2... 3...

All I want is to be someone's true blue,
though someone's baby blue would be alright,
and I wish someone would boost me up
to that saddle that carried me high.

Choose me and feed me flakes from the sky,
and dress me with leaves that you grew.
And finally, instead of all those letters,
why can't I just stick with U?

Winter is Coming

Winter comes.

She hunts,
crouches low with eyes
on the prize of a soul,
hungry for resignation.

Her cool breathe escapes her lips,
leaves chills on hopeless hearts,
spits white-whipped promises.

It is enticement to stay forever,
wrapped up in ice and stillness
like a corpse in a basement morgue
lies on cold concrete waiting for fire.

If there was even the hope of hope,
the dream of dreaming again while sleeping
instead of wasting night
-       after night -
-       after night -
in the black bleakness of more lost time...

If there was energy to move toward the horizon
where the sun lies waiting to hold memories

in his warm arms once more,
like long before,
I would go to his bed ten leaps from the moon
and let him spoon me.

But there is nothing left of the universe,
and the world is a wasteland,
for invincibility is the thread,
and invulnerability the needle,
that sews the clothes of children,
and acceptance and awareness
create the calloused hands that craft
the small graves of the nearly gone.

Last night,
I knelt staring down into lake water;
the reflection back was who I was
silhouetted in moonlight,
the illusion of years never lived
alive in the dark of the night,
promises of years to come
hidden behind the morning sun,
then sleeping.

I may not see her waken.

I may just find her tempting fate,
and in that moment,
I could lie beside her

and accept that she will not move
from her fetal coil,
back turned toward me now.

Once, she held tight like a mother holds blood.

It is not quite Summer,
yet it does not feel still like Spring.

It is nearly warm enough,
but only nearly,
to believe in something greater
than what was achieved,
but the tree limbs are lined with rings
-        and rings -
-        and rings -
but not one branch wears one of gold,
and fading leaves fall
to decaying piles on mounds
of dirt and browning grass,
parched for lack of rain.

No nutrients remain in the soil.

They are elsewhere,
feeding the living,
long ago giving up on arms
once reaching for telephone wires
now broken from storms,

lying like dead snakes in silence.

Even if the years screamed
to breach the uneven crumbling
brick walls of a looming tomb,
Summer simply never
answers a whisper.

And Winter comes.

ATHAZAGORAPHOBIA3

When we were young, we laughed over
concotions
of rum and vodka and things that give you wings
and a little of this, a little of that
in the sunshine, hair wet from days in the pool,
visiting every city we could, flirting
with death and strangers asking our names.

We sat by bonfires with cheap beer,
gossiped, speculated, and worried about
what might become when life took over,
but we promised each other a long future
forever, us, always forever;
now, on still and quiet Friday nights,
you tell your brand new friends forever,
and I ask myself what did I do?

What did I do?

What did I do?

2.

When I was young, impressionable, asking

47

who, what, why, where, when, and how about
the world,
the answers evasive and absent, like Dad,
I looked to you for sustenance, mind a sponge.
I looked to each man that came and ignored me
to teach me things my Dad never did,
to give me the parents my friends had,
but they sent me away, took you, left me
between
love and hate and the wondering why.

We were best friends; we were Thelma and
Louise,
steep cliffs always one step ahead; we
dove, drove, time and again, hoping that
our life would be hopeful in morning.

In mourning, I ask, what did I do?

      What did I do?

      What did I do?

3.

If I did something wrong, passed judgment on
you
while in the gentle arms of a loving God,

succumbed to your will when it was not your
will,
made eyes at our waiter at new restaurants,
in my red dress I would not let you take off,
drove too fast, swore in front of your Mom,
I died to know why my phone became
still and quiet – trees before a tornado,
our heartbeats when the towers came down,
a Buddhist monk in solemn meditation,
no quick vibration like a kick drum,
no ring like the cracked Liberty Bell,
quiet and still – silence and whispers,
and painful questions: what did I do?

What did I do?

What did I do?

A Bear's Feeding

Bears feed
in water currents
where the morning sun
is dying,
filled with long life
and invisible fire.

I have not been
on that journey.

21 Ways to Look at Water

Grief comes in ebbs and flows,
a million waves of waiting.

I have been there,
lost in the dark of the ocean,
set adrift a thousand miles from land.

My Mother is my rowboat torn with holes.
Long gone friends are anchors when I sink.
Your death will be my unquenchable thirst
in a world of saltwater.

The eventuality rests in peaceful stillness,
yet, it will rise like a tidal wave
and descend one day from a clear, blue sky.

At your wake,
I will rise, and I will fall.
I will become like the tides
touching shore and fading out again.

I will swallow whole the sand
left from decomposing seashells.
I will become lightning glass,
sharp and dangerous

and beautiful.

Until that day, the stormiest day,
the day of utter darkness
lit briefly by the lightning
of my memories with you,
we will swim until we drown.